# Tintoretto

Virgil Mocanu

ABBEY LIBRARY
LONDON

Tin

toretto

Translated from Romanian as published by
MERIDIANE PUBLISHING HOUSE
Bucharest, 1977
under the original title of
TINTORETTO
by
VIRGIL MOCANU

Translated into English by
CAROL KORMOS

It is the good fortune of Jacopo Robusti, called Tintoretto, that enthusiastic Romanticists and discerning critics have integrated his work in the flux of an objective process typical of our twentieth century: the desire to discover, legitimate and relaunch forerunners. Frequently forgotten, onesidedly interpreted and sometimes unconsidered, predecessors suddenly become "cases" serving as conceptual or iconographic arguments pleading for certain trends, thereby acquiring the status of a spiritual mainstay, of a recurrent attitude. A glorious heredity is an explicit confirmation of the fact that the crucial questions of human awareness travel across the ages and always succeed in expressing themselves in a specific style that is linked to historical demands.

It is the same with Tintoretto, although with him it would perhaps be more true to say that the message of his art is "fructified" in the modern, and possibly more appropriate, perspective. This is so because, while organically belonging to a structure whose meanings and effects we now realize more clearly, the artist was an echo of his time and also succeeded in surpassing the limits and impositions of an agitated age.

Early 16th-century Europe was changing fast. The numerous and far-reaching political, economic and social transformations were increasingly felt in the mobile sphere of spiritual life. Mature Renaissance, in the modern historiographical meaning of the term, cleansed of its exaggerated romanticist and idealistic halo, was at its climax. However, this apex implicitly also marked the beginning of a transition, of a definite opening towards a new historical stage, possibly less spectacular, but of at least equal importance to the destiny of art and culture.

Divided by internal struggles and the assault of France and Spain, the great powers that had taken shape at the end of the 15th century, Italy was in a general political decline. Tintoretto, though, had the good luck of being born in free, liberal Venice. The proud city, with its original political, economic and civic concepts, fully enjoying all the advantages it derived from its contacts with the sea, with the rich and mysterious East, and cultivating a hybrid, and therefore highly productive, Christian but unorthodox spiritual life, had become the last defender of independence, resisting foreign attack and the offensive of Catholic fanaticism resurrected by the Reformation. Venice was unfavourable, and even hostile, to the institution of the Inquisition in Italy (1542), to the fallacious decisions of the Council of Trent, to the Counter-Reformation and the Jesuits. This accounted for its reputation as "the city of liberty," which was acknowledged by all contemporaries and reflects an objective reality. In a country forced to its knees by foreign powers, Venice alone remained free. And in order to remain free, the city used force, diplomacy, money and compromise. "Venice means the liberty of Italy," wrote Alessandro Borgia. Pope Pius V called it "the splendour and glory of Italy !", and the doge Tommaso Mocenigo, "the only republic, the only part and only corner of Italy that has remained free." "Today, there is no liberty in the world except in Venice," said Gaspare Contarini. Tintoretto's most ardent partisan and admirer, Pietro Aretino, wrote in 1530: "Universal homeland ! The shelter of the hounded !" Pathetic effusion? Certainly, but one matching reality, even if we carefully weigh the relative meaning of liberty and independence.

Simultaneously, the *Serenissima Republica* developed an intellectual and artistic life of great force and originality, deriving from a very particular development of elements taken from the concept and language of the "grand Renaissance style." Tintoretto therefore grew up in a fully structured climate, the sum of successive, and conclusive accumulations. Venetian art now represented the totality of the means of expression resulting from the work of the local masters, but also incorporating the contribution of the other Italian schools, some of which had by now exhausted their strength, and also the gains of the great Northern experiments, of the Flemish school of Van Eyck, of Petrus Christus and Antonello da Messina, but also of the German school, of Dürer, Schongauer, Altdorfer, or Baldung Grien. Moreover, Venetian art now had a receptivity originating in its evolutionary process and requiring non-decadent if not novel solutions.

Tintoretto was the beneficiary of local traditions as stimulating as they were inhibitive because they embodied Jacopo, Gentile and Giovanni Bellini, Carpaccio, Mantegna, Antonello da Messina, Giorgione and Bassano as well as Titian. However, his destiny as a painter also stood under the sign of the great Florentines — although to him Michelangelo represented all of them — and of the scepticism which provoked the "mannerist crisis." Analysing Tintoretto's work today with discernment and impartiality, we see it as an original and homogenous synthesis blending the three conceptual and stylistic trends. The decisive element, though, marking its creative essence, is his unique, powerful personality.

We know practically nothing of his early years. Born in 1518, at the end of September or beginning of October [1], Tintoretto is first mentioned in a document in 1539, in a will speaking of *Mastro Giacomo depentor* domiciled in San Cassiano Square in Venice. This is the document which has given birth to the legend that he spent ten days as a pupil in Titian's studio, a story recorded by the artist's biographer, Ridolfi, with some caution ("... it is said that ..."), but until recently retold with evident enthusiasm by all successive writers. Essentially romantic, the story served to give the impression that Titian was jealous of his disciple of genius and Tintoretto was obstinate, proud, very well aware of his worth, a cliché that was readily accepted because of its sensational character. Although questioned by contemporary critics, the episode has been accepted by the well-known expert Giuseppe De Logu, because it might justify another legend intended to explain the sources of Tintoretto's art, or at least the particular features of his style. And it also originates with Ridolfi, who wrote that Tintoretto had posted a sign in his studio saying: "*Il disegno de Michel'Angelo, ed il colorito di Tiziano.*"

This formula sought to provide an explanation by way of simplification, simultaneously putting forward two different theoretical premises. Being linked to two well-established personalities, Tintoretto's work was thereby given an acceptable interpretation. One must not forget that Michelangelo was the titan who dominated his time with his expressive force and sweeping passion, and that his work, continuing the great classical style, resulted in the appearance of imitators. Titian was the genuine representative of the Venetian dimension, of colour. He introduced "the large manner" and had an impressive reputation, being a Count Palatine of the Holy Roman Empire, the painter of François I of France, Charles V, Philip II and Pope Paul III. The two men represented the peaks of the ideal of the late Renaissance, much more so than the originality of other artists — the years after 1520 saw the rise of Tuscan and Roman mannerism — or the fame of Raphael. The formula gave an explanation as to the style of Tintoretto's original work, which some considered paradoxical, and also an infallible justification. Every imitator would have been happy with the reflected glory of the two titans. Tintoretto was not, and could not be, because he was the type of man who is aware of his worth and therefore does not accept subordination. He had created a style, he wanted to demonstrate this, and succeeded in doing so, without denying or denigrating his predecessors. The legend illustrates Tintoretto's good fortune of having been born into an age of scepticism in which he successfully promoted a generous and active human ideal, and also his handicap of being considered a successor who was only admitted into an exceptional hierarchy for his similitude with his predecessors. Today, though, nobody can accept this evidently prejudiced view any longer. An examination of the work of the three artists by aesthetic, semantic and stylistic criteria reveals a different reality. As a matter of fact, the contemporaries of Tintoretto did not consider him an imitator. To do so would indeed have been difficult

---

[1]. In his *Il riposto della pittura e della scultura*, published in 1584, Borghini suggests that Tintoretto was born in 1524. Another biographer, Carlo Ridolfi, in his *Vita de Giacopo Robusti*, published in Venice in 1624, believes the year of birth was 1512. The death certificate of the Church of San Marziale states that the artist was seventy-five (1518—1594).

when his work produced so many passionate debates and provoked such strong opposition, so many conflicting opinions. However, all his adepts and adversaries testified to the great fascination of his work. Even the eclectic, solemn and fastidious Vasari, who held that Tintoretto's success was due to accident and rapid execution rather than the correct application of classical rules, acknowledged that the artist was "*il piu terribile cervello de la pittura.*"

Actually, at least in the first period of his career, Tintoretto's formula did not differ very much from the examples of his two forerunners. The modern examination of his work, particularly of the few but significant preparatory drawings and sketches, has spotlighted the influence of Michelangelo and Titian on the young artist. The drawings point to familiarity with Michelangelo's models, and possibly to direct contact with the work of the Florentine master during a trip Tintoretto probably made to Rome in 1545 or 1546, a theory put forward by N. Pevsner and Pallucchini which was rejected by H. Tietze. It is also thought that he worked after copies, especially those made by Daniele de Volterra in 1557. Palluchini, though, demonstrates that Tintoretto's drawings were made before Volterra's copies and believes Tintoretto worked after the originals or, which is an even more attractive hypothesis, after antique models. As a matter of fact, Tintoretto was reputed to be good at drawing even when he was still a young man. Borghini said the great artist drew "*tutte le cose buone de Venezia*" as well as the sculptures of the great Florentines and of his friend Jacopo Sansovino, while Ridolfi recorded a significant statement according to which Tintoretto believed that one "could not become a painter without drawing every day." Tintoretto was the only Venetian artist who introduced drawing as a compulsory subject of study in his workshop, being convinced that it was an essential component of pictorial structure. And although his vision was purely pictorial, even his developing concepts were similar in this respect with those of Michelangelo.

As to the contribution of the "Titian formula" in Tintoretto's synthesis, one has to accept the idea from a critical viewpoint in the sense given to it by Tintoretto's mature work. Ridolfi had launched an attractive legend. Borghini denied it by saying that Tintoretto had studied colour in nature, while admitting that there was a possibility of his having worked after Titian's pictures. We know that Tintoretto acquired sketches of the master after the latter's death, but he did so after 1576 when he already was an established personality and had a fully formed style of his own. In our view, the similitudes are due to the fact that both painters were Venetians, that is artists of colour and atmosphere, and in his first phase, up to the year 1545, Tintoretto was linked to local tradition. The truth is that for most people Venetian painting was and still is identified with Titian. This is the origin of the prejudiced view, which survived for a long time, that Tintoretto was a direct emanation of the spirit and manner of Titian, a gifted disciple of his and no more. The contemporary view repudiates this assertion which justifies the enthusiasm for the great Venetian master but wrongs the younger artist, and unjustifiably so. Simplifying the question of influences in order to remain impartial, we might therefore join Zabeo in saying that "Tintoretto was nobody's disciple."

As a matter of fact, the idea of the two titans contributing to the formation of Tintoretto's style also has theoretical implications making for a possible conciliation of, at the time, opposed views on art. In the context of the epoch this attempt was not new. In 1548, Paolo Pino had published a *Dialogo della pittura* the essential purpose of which was similar. An empirical yet correct intuition saw the difference between two apparently contradictory attitudes which might be defined as *sculptural* and *pictorial*. The motto "Michelangelo's drawing and Titian's colour" therefore played a precise role in Ridolfi's argument, but also in Tintoretto's work, and this might explain, if only in part, the process shaping a pictorial language of incomparable originality.

In addition to these external factors, there was a decisive one, and its decisive nature was due to conceptual and stylistic implications: the assertion of mannerism. "In the year 1523, Francesco Mazzola of Parma, called 'Il Parmigianino', sat down before a convex mirror and painted an astonishing portrait." [2] This was the first explicit

---

**2.** Gustav René Hocke, *Die Welt als Labyrinth*, Rowohlt Taschenbuch Verlag GmbH, Hamburg, 1957.

affirmation of the mannerist formula in all its complexity, a formula which had an impact on the 16th. century and many European artistic, trends up to the modern age.

Elements of mannerist thinking and procedures appeared at the time in Venetian painting, and particularly with Tintoretto, in tune with an objective process of contagion and with the dialectic of changes occurring in the spirit of the epoch. Compared to the characteristic expressions of mannerism, Tintoretto's work certainly is not an archetype, although Hocke considers the artist, next to his disciple of genius, El Greco, as the greatest mannerist painter. However, the qualitative proportion is inverted when the analysis shifts to the examination of autonomous, intrinsic values. There is no doubt whatever that Pontormo, Rosso Fiorentino, Parmigianino and Giulio Romano are more mannerist in the handling of certain subjects, spiritual structures, procedures, sigla or *concette*, but Tintoretto's primacy derives from the force of his personality that cannot be ascribed to a certain trend because he refuses the convenience of a recipe and the servitude inherent in the utilization of an approved model. This does not mean that in 1545—1550 mannerist influences, dissolved in the synthesis of his own art, failed to contribute to the shaping of a specific and unitary style.

The effects of these cross-currents of influences and temptations, and of the assertion of his own personality were already visible in the work of the young artist. Tintoretto was a merry and very lively person. Vasari writes that he was fond of music. which he played well, a bent coinciding with his contemporaries' liking for entertainment, music and the theatre, which he depicted in several canvases featuring musical allegories. In addition to an *Allegory of Music*, for a long time attributed to Giorgione, a quite excusable mistake, there is the remarkable picture *Rivalry between the Muses and the Pierians* [3] both of them pretexts for a splendid display of nudes, costumes, musical instruments and symbols placed in rather conventional landscapes. From the pictorial viewpoint, these paintings evince kinship with "the large manner" Titian had inaugurated and with a style euphemistically named "modified classicism", actually a result of the incipient spiritual crisis marking the decline of the Renaissance.

The years 1540—1548 were a fertile period, particularly as regards accumulations and decantations, projecting the premises of originality, although Tintoretto also resorted to the inevitable conventional formulae, and it outlined the principal themes of his future work, based on mythology and biblical legends. His commissioned religious pictures did not yet excel by originality or variety; they were part of a classical repertoire used by all artists, and should be taken as exercises required for the definition of his own equations. Between 1537 and 1541 alone, Tintoretto sold eleven canvases featuring the *Holy Family*, a subject in great demand and linked to the tradition of the *Sacra conversazione*.

The artist gradually began to be marked by the rather swift transformations he experienced and which pushed apparently unchanging values into a realm of confusion and uncertainty whose latency was increased by the evolution of historical events. Deception already seems to have affected the personality of the artist, and his orientation towards dramatic subjects, involving essential elements of the human condition, emphasizes this irreversible process. The consequences of this transformation went beyond the bounds of a simple stylistic suffusion. This might be explained by that controversial journey to Rome, dated 1545—1546, implying direct contact with the ideas of the age, but also with the work of Michelangelo. *The Last Judgement* no longer was an occasion for stupefaction or ecclesiastic scandal. It had established itself in the public consciousness, and its significance surpassed the dimensions of an interest aroused by a non-canonical and unusual painting. Aretino, wrote Michelangelo in April 1541: "In *The Last Judgement* I saw the representation of horror, and realizing that you have experienced it, my eyes filled with tears.." This is an astonishingly modern view, intuiting the essence of the message, and comparable to Stendhal's reaction three centuries later: "Michelangelo overwhelms the imagination with the burden of misfortune. We no longer have the strength of courage. Misfortune fills the whole soul." This soul, filled

---

[3]. The picture represents the nine daughters of king Pieros of Macedonia, the competitors of the Muses, transformed into magpies in punishment for their insolence. Two magpies are therefore placed on two corners of the canvas. One has a score in its beak, and other a lute.

with horror and overwhelmed by misfortune, was typical of the spirit of an age standing on a brink and having the vague feeling of passing through an epochal crisis. The human message of Michelangelo's fresco, the tension and dramatism of the most explicit parable of existence painted so far, affected the concept and manner of Tintoretto.

Probably the most significant work in this context is *The Last Supper* painted in 1547 for the church of San Marcuola. The date of this picture, which inaugurated a cycle of *Last Suppers* painted throughout the career of the Venetian master, is clearly indicated by the inscription on the stool in the centre of the scene: MDXXXX/VII: A DI XXVII / AGOSTO / I TEMPO / DE MISER / ISE / PO MORANDE / LO ET CONPAGNI, that is 1547, on the 27th of August, at the time of *messer* Isepo Morandelo and his companions. Employing realistic elements that had been used before, but doing it in a new and significant way for a traditional compositional scheme recalling the Byzantine model on a line parallel to the viewer, the artist produced a novel expression filled with the tension of revelation. Although the texture of the portraits derives from the traditions of the Renaissance, the quality of the light and its distribution, the incipient dynamics of gesture and composition, the unusual anatomical logic, and the mixture of vigour and mannerist delicacy draw attention to great originality. The human drama is embodied by the multitude of stances around the central personality and generates a new affective universe. This was particularly important for subsequent developments. The *Miracle of the Slave, (St. Mark Rescuing a Slave)*, painted for the Scuola Grande di San Marco [4], confirmed the establishment of an exacerbated inner tension, although the lesson of Venetian colourism and Florentine design were still dominant, blurring the novelty of the formula. A display of anatomical studies and foreshortenings, the picture records the elements of light and chromatics of a carefully staged dramatism justifying the praise of Paolo Pino, Andrea Calmo and Aretino. It was this picture which drew public attention to Tintoretto, although, according to Ridolfi and Boschini, there was strong opposition to its acceptance by the confraternity. The scene represents one of the posthumous miracles of St. Mark, when he saved a slave who had been condemned for having made a pilgrimage to the holy relics in Venice from torture. Tumultuous movement, the *deus ex macchina* intervention of the Saint and the composition based on the opposition of the diagonal lines lend dynamism and tension to the scene. This was a concept astonishing the visual habits of the Venetians, a new pictorial formula modifying the role of space and light. It was the result of long, consistent experiment. The spectacular stage effects will be understood if we remember the taste of the century for the theatre, its propensity to see the world as a stage, which, as Arnold Hauser remarks, was a way of eluding reality, but also the artist's liking for the spectacle. Some of his contemporaries, among them Ridolfi in his *Le meraviglie dell'arte*, described the minute "stagings" Tintoretto made with little models of wax and clay, dressing them up and setting them up in little cardboard houses, lighted from the most surprising angles by candles or torches, the forerunners of surrealist or metaphysical puppets hung from ceilings to study the anamorphoses and the play of shadows. The mannerist procedure of manipulating light, of multiple sources with scenic functions made its way in Venice thanks to Tintoretto. The Renaissance perspective gained velocity and was compressed according to nascent laws comprising all the longings of that strange century straining between the discovery of new worlds and the rejection of logical reality.

A man of his age, Tintoretto was the beneficiary of an unprecedented situation and of frequently baffling solutions. He certainly must have known the phantastic, even hallucinating treatise of the Venetian monk Francesco Colonna suggestively entitled *Hypnerotomachia Poliphili*, in which the author advocates a compelling, unreal, unrealistic but attractive architecture. A contemporary of Sebastiano Serlio of Bologna, another theorician of architecture, Tintoretto must have studied, if only out of purely professional curiosity, the volumes of *Il libro d'architettura*, just as he must have known the studies and plans of Palladio, who built the church of San Giorgio Maggiore, for which the artist painted one of the most phantastic and striking *Suppers*. A friend and portraitist of the celebrated Jacopo Sansovino, Tintoretto reproduced elements and even entire groups of buildings made by the most interesting Venetian architect in his canvases.

---

[4]. There were many charitable religious brotherhoods, called *scuole*, in Venice. Membership was a coveted honour.

The lesson of Renaissance perspective in a painting like *Christ Washing the Feet of the Apostles* and the foreshortening in the *Miracle of the Slave* therefore express different attitudes separating two aesthetic ideals, two epochs and their ideals, and not simply an antagonism of geometric elements.

Although emotionally involved in the drama of the Venetian artist, we can now be impartial spectators at this distance, from all the passions, achievements and insuccesses of that century of tensions and contradictions, and judge the value and significance of the mutation taking place in Tintoretto's concept. The historical setting turned Tintoretto's work into the point of confluence of the most characteristic pressures exercised by a new human and artistic perspective upon the Renaissance ideals which he incorporated in a final synthesis without denying their profound essence. Possibly less concerned with cultural implications, but fully involved in the certitudes and doubts of a new plastic universe, he defined himself by a frenetic thirst of work. His was a permanent and tenacious contest with the limits of the human condition. Today, just as four centuries ago, his *fa presto* is strikingly astonishing. Moving inventively and with rare self-assurance in a whole universe of commissioned themes and subjects, he fulfilled his destiny with the only care of respecting what for him and through him was an objective and implacable commandment of European art. Equally gifted when painting sensual mythological scenes and religious tragedies, portraits and large compositions, driven by what Zanetti called "furious enthusiasm", Tintoretto created his own paradox: considered by most as a mystic painter, he actually proclaimed the most profound and genuine secular concepts of man and the universe.

Using a procedure explicitly formulated by modern critics, but already existing in the work of the Renaissance artists, we make a distinction between the literary subject and the real content of the work clothed in metaphor, symbol and allegory. In so doing, we have the revelation of a Tintoretto who amplifies the lesson of Michelangelo's titanism and of sensual, pantheist and heathen Venetianism with new means and in a new philosophical climate. In those years of the initial battle between Catholicism and the Reformation, religious subjects could obviously not be avoided, but Tintoretto transformed them into pretexts, all of which served his purpose, for big, dramatic scenes of spiritual tension with an appealing human message. Confused and complicated biblical or hagiographical legends were often simplified and clarified by linking their meaning to the human essence dissimulated by the canonical discourse.

Historical developments constantly influenced Tintoretto's life and work. His artistic universe, concepts and manner took shape in the years of the long and inconclusive Council of Trent, the consequences of which had a great impact on the spirit and history of Europe. There still is a unilateral and mistaken trend linked to certain anecdotes seeking to represent Tintoretto as an artist of the Counter-Reformation. In this attempt, aspects whose implications require an impartial and perceptive analysis are simplified, and real structure and content are replaced by a flamboyant and convenient mechanical formula. Tintoretto certainly could not be and actually was not an atheist, but like all Venetian intellectuals in the years of religious disputes having an ideological and pragmatic purport, he was not interested in, and even less receptive to, the excessive zeal of dogmatic Catholicism. A simple collation of his paintings with the principles laid down by the Council of Trent produces conclusive evidence. His work does not comprise and does not proclaim the themes and ideas recommended by the Council which were officially formulated in a rhetoric canonical repertory and subsequently exploited ad *infinitum*. The well-informed and straightforward critic Giuseppe De Logu said: "In Venice, the Counter-Reformation has two names: Veronese and Sarpi". And he adduced iconographic and theoretical evidence bearing out his statement.

The realistic, iconoclastic way in which he represented his personages astonished Tintoretto's contemporaries. Their reaction was not always favourable, and this is not at all surprising in view of the ideal of serene elegance promoted so far. Still confused, but unacceptable, the notions *meraviglia* and *stupore*, so dear to the mannerists, were met with prudent reserve. Assimilated and taken up as a formula, the constrained vitalism of the Venetian's work was invoked and used as a stylistic argument by Baroque art, although the conceptual difference demonstrates a simple process of mechanical resumption and enlargement of superficial procedures. What actually happened was that Tintoretto, setting out from new philosophical and aesthetic positions, again launched the proud postulate of Antiquity the Renaissance had adopted, "Man is the measure of all things and the centre of the Universe", thereby making his own contribution to the establishment of a novel ontological perspective in consonance with the aims and views of his century. This is one, but not the only reason why in his work we discern questions rather than answers, aspirations, and not conclusions, disturbing premonitions, but also hopes for the salvation of mankind.

The years between the first *Supper* and the *Miracle of the Slave*, and the overwhelming pictorial cycle for the Scuola di San Rocco, that is the period between 1547 and 1564, were most significant for the way in which Tintoretto's art crystallized its fundamental data. His subsequent work in all its dramatic complexity already exists *in nuce* in the tensional gradation to be found in the astonishing exercises on the subjects of the three great themes whose confluence forms his artistic universe. Lay subjects, ever-present throughout his work as a dominant feature, mythological subjects, used for their symbolical values, and religious subjects taken from the Old and New Testaments are subordinated to a single concept ruled by humanism comprising a new significance, a new human perspective, different from the one that had been accepted so far.

Without artificial exaggeration of the logic to be found in Tintoretto's paintings, we can discern in them two distinctive, but not antinomic or irreconcilable manners, intentionally used for two categories of subjects in a compensatory yet different way.

Mythology, long since established as a poetic code needed to explain a cosmogony transformed into a legendary epic, furnishes accepted allegories and symbols, but also pretexts for literary allusions involving the formal elegance and the sensualism typical of Venetian art and expanding the ideal of physical beauty. Subjects taken from the Old Testament and relating to domestic, often licentious stories that are unimportant as to ontological implications, are assimilated with mythological subjects by virtue of their similar transcendental and apocryphal condition, and treated in the same pictorial manner.

The second category, having a particular, distinctive style, is made up of stories, accepted as being real or possible, from the New Testament and the hagiographic legends, as well as the chapters of the Old Testament comprising prophecies of revelation and sacrifice. The subjects are set in scenarios in which the protagonists frequently have an attested identity, drawn from documentary sources, and not anthropomorphic myths. The compositions are dramatic, reflecting not only a new concept of the human condition as it was taking shape in the century of mannerism and escapism, but also an impetuous desire of surpassing it. Hence the often exacerbating spiritual tension, the realism and pathetism of the personages, the rehtoric, symbolic attitude characterizing the second manner which definitely established itself after the year 1560.

Returning to the question of the influences exercized on the artist in his early years, we shall find that there is a solution of conciliation between the Venetian Renaissance as represented by Titian and the passionate vitalism of Michelangelo's art. The two planes combine according to a strictly pictorial logic, clearly rejecting hybridism and stylistic ambiguity, propounding a single, unitary, eloquent and original way of expression.

Painted in the same period, probably between 1550 and 1560, several pictures selected as minimal iconographic arguments will serve to demonstrate the idea of the two styles in Tintoretto's work.

The miraculous descent of the *deus ex macchina* type in the canvas *St. Augustine Healing the Plague-stricken* suggests a timidly expressed but developing spiritual tension. The realistic representation of human beings, the eloquence of their attitudes and their often rhetorical symbolism, the dynamics of the compositional diagonal lines and the spiritual vigour clothed in pathetic gestures belong to a zone of dramatism having profound human implications. Michelangelo's influence is evident in the anatomic structure, but the turgescence of the muscular mass is considerably tempered by the mannerist interpretation of the silhouettes which are lengthened in order to emphasize the spiritual quality of the scene. The composition, too, is mannerist. It uses the accelerated perspective by introducing sliding planes and an apparently immaterial architectural background in keeping with a scenographic formula that was very popular and widely used in the 16th. century. The carefully manipulated lighting is also mannerist. It creates an unreal atmosphere of anxiety. Material existence is explicitly separated from spiritual revelation, and this division is underlined by grandiloquent dominant gestures and pictorial artifice. The picture has traces of Tuscan design in its mannerist interpretation, but also of Venetian colourism worked in "the large manner." The meaning of the general expression, though, is new, and close to our century, and the ectoplasmic figures in the background, flashing anthropomorphic shapes, look like deriving from 20th. century surrealistic morphology.

Total human involvement with the pictorial essence has set its mark on Tintoretto's work. Successive accumulations are crystallized in a unitary and clear-cut concept. And the common denominator of this profoundly human attitude might well be termed "the obsession with revelation."

The spiritual support and the great chance of the human condition resides in this ontological revelation, in the possibility of knowledge and understanding that could lead to a stage beyond doubt, agitation, resignation and suffering. For Tintoretto, the miracle itself, unreal and fascinating, remains an exterior event, an anecdote he uses as a pretext to stage a spectacular, symbolic show. Really important is the essence of the conflict, of the relations between the principles that are involved. Thus a new axiological system is outlined, based on the elements of a new, more sincere and more realistic humanism than the one promoted thus far by the Renaissance, more sincere and realistic because it finds room for creative doubt generated by the experience of profound psychological probing. Setting out from this surprisingly modern premise, Tintoretto developed it in his entire mature work which became his artistic and human *credo*. Assuming an overwhelming responsibility for his artistic and pictorial concept, Tintoretto felt definitely and fully involved in his creative work. That is why he often included himself as a knowledgeable spectator in his pictures, not motivated by frivolous professional pride but rather with the explicit intention of emphasizing the real meaning of his message.

This obsession with revelation transforms the *Presentation of the Virgin in the Temple* into a spectacular mystery with a wealth of allusions and of a pictorial power that heightens the effect of *stupore*. Vasari saw the painting in 1568 in the church of Santa Maria dell'Orto, where it is to this day. "It is a finished work, the best executed and most successful painting in the church," he wrote with enthusiasm. The Florentine critic's judgement seems fully justified, despite the praise showered on the work in the course of several centuries. Spectacular effects and inventiveness characterize the subject, also treated by other Venetian painters, Cima da Conegliano and Titian, adding an unprecedented, dramatic accent to it which is linked to the spiritual make-up of the mannerist century. The opposition between the compositional diagonals and the lighting tend to isolate a unique personality, the key of the entire scene: small Mary who, as yet unaware of the tragic implications of her human destiny, experiences the fascinating solemnity. Non-initiated witnesses of this ontological mystery, the other participants do not have any anecdotic or pictorial relief, except for the biblical personage at the head of the stairs and the woman in the foreground. Her rhetoric, eloquent gesture reveals the meaning of the scene and its protagonist. This gesture, although assuming different forms, is a recurrent feature of the artist's work. Always impetuous, it is an affective pointer, a pictorial sign entitling us to speak of a "Tintoretto gesture." The spectator's attention is arrested, and directed to the intention of the artist. The message is decoded, revealing a different, though not antinomic universe that is essentially unlike the immediately visual one. The lighting, diverging from the tradition stipulating a single, unifying source, works from a perspective which, aware of the relativity of the term and its inherent dangers, we might call "pre-cinematographic"; it emphasizes or blurs, thereby annulling the classical, equal relief typical of the Renaissance. This, then, is the mannerist universe, an ambiguous mixture of legend, enigma, irreality and *meraviglia*. The silhouettes integrate with the new canon, they become longer, aspiring to the imponderable nature of a higher spiritual condition. Structures with a new meaning are emerging. An unprecedented pictorial reality is establishing itself. Between the figure of Mary, fragile and yet authoritarian because she embodies a principle, and that of the mysterious and imposing High Priest, there suddenly appears an obelisk. It bears a cryptic, probably imaginary message in which hieroglyphs take us into the Eastern regions of the biblical legends. A traditional signpost for the localization of the action, a literary allusion and conventional mark, the obelisk in Tintoretto's painting gives us the certainty that the artist was an intellectual who had assimilated not only mannerist procedures, but also the creative spirit. He also used the motif in *Christ Washing the*

*Feet of the Apostles*, in the Prado, and later in the *Crucifixion* in the Scuola di San Rocco. The relation that has been found between the obelisk and the Christ cycle seems to confirm that we are dealing with a geographical sign based on the simple and efficient principle of association: obelisk = the ancient East.

Yet another architectural element invested with symbolical functions forcefully separates the planes of action and spotlights the allusive intention of the image. That element is the staircase. It becomes a constantly recurrent sign of Tintoretto, dividing reality from the ideal, standing between the material existence of the characters and their desire for a different spiritual quality. Thanks to Tintoretto, this pictorial artifice, employed mainly because it is spectacular, changes its dimensions and acquires a new scope, becoming a metaphor generating mental associations and emotional suggestions. The flight of stairs forms a dizzy rising spiral suggesting an energy in space accompanying the spiritual uplift to which the protagonist submits. Certifying the novelty of these solutions, and particularly the interplay of chiaroscuro introduced three centuries later by the impressionists under the impact of photographic inventions, Wölfflin says that this painting validates the originality of manipulation for the sake of symbolic finality Tintoretto had inaugurated. Its scenic relationship and feeling for the postulated plastic space therefore made it the manifesto and prototype of a new and surprisingly modern concept.

*Deposition* bears the mark of the essential change in the artist's pictorial course in the direction of the zone of exacerbated spiritual tension. Its intensive expressiveness was a starting point for a determined departure from everything that had formed the traditional fund of 16th. century art. Once again quoting, and agreeing with, Wölfflin, we believe that this is one of Tintoretto's most striking pictures. The tragic character of the scene, its profoundly human meaning are highlighted by a new pictorial essence, lacking the international ambiguity and rhetoric to be found in the celebrated mannerist paintings of Pontormo and Rosso Fiorentino. Compared with them, the originality of the restrained humanism in Tintoretto's picture becomes even more evident. The dynamic in-depth orientation of the diagonal lines represented by the bodies of Christ and Mary dominates the entire image, and the carefully arranged lighting amplifies the emotional climate of the great tragedy. This is a scene freed from its traditional meaning, becoming an explicit affirmation that reflects the artist's non-mystical if not atheistic views. The body of Christ, taken from the cross, dissolves in the symbolic shadow of death, producing the feeling of participation in a mystery in which only matter, a body still strong in its transience, is doomed to disappearance. The second affective and plastic centre of the scene is produced by the lighting to create another pictorial and symbolic effect. Mary is no longer the serene and self-assured child she was in the *Presentation*. She participates in the final drama. Her profoundly human sorrow leaves no room for any other feelings. The paroxism of the characters, expressed by their attitudes, points to a very modern perspective resumed by the Baroque and launched anew by Romanticism. The interplay of chiaroscuro, the vigorous design underlined by the manipulation of coloured matter flashing in rapid accents and the attention paid to significant detail all help to transform a routine subject into an explicit parable. The classical canon is displaced by the surge of expressive force. The ideal of nearly two centuries of assurance and equilibrium is challenged by questions and uneasiness, elements subsequently taken over by European art in its confrontation with its human and aesthetic destiny.

The coherent and passionate pictorial discourse, initiated in the years 1550—1560 and gradually transformed into a unitary and unmistakable style, continues to comprise brilliant experiments conducted in the good Venetian tradition and under the influence of spectacular mannerist artifices. Clever and elegant pieces of virtuosity, these tonal orchestrations are impregnated with a profound chromatic sonority, with voluptuous colour and light organically incorporated in matter. The subjects are taken from a mythological and biblical repertoire that does not offend the dominant dogma, but they make it possible, and even necessary, to have a free treatment suffused with the typically Venetian pagan sensualism as yet unaltered by the prudish bigotry of the Counter-Reformation. The absence of dramatic substance is compensated by a brilliant display of virtuosity. Tintoretto was a contemporary of the elegant chronicler of Venetian feasts, Paolo Veronese, and the latter's impact on him, or possibly the fact that they belonged to the same spiritual matrix, contributed to the definition of a unique moment in 16th-century Italian art: a meeting and competition from which the great 18th-century Venetians Guardi, Canaletto, Longhi, Piazzetta and Tiepolo, and all European art derived great benefit.

Still sufficiently "classical" to win over his contemporaries, sufficiently "impressionistic" and "romantic" to anger them, and highly modern, for which reason we lay claim to him today, Tintoretto calls and leads us to a new universe, that of the proud Venetian openly battling on a territory so far authoritatively ruled by Titian, and demonstrating that he is capable of at least equal performances and, what is more, of bigger feats which others cannot perform or even fathom.

Let us consider two of the six pictures known as the "Old Testament" scenes in the Prado, Madrid, by Tintoretto; according to Borghini and Ridolfi they were commissioned by Spain's Philip II, and according to Palomino bought by Velázquez in 1649 as "ceiling paintings." Two of these ceiling panels are typical of Tintoretto's art at that time, *Joseph and Potiphar's Wife* and *The Finding of Moses*. Painted about 1555, during the period in which his style crystallized and he made his great experiments the cycle is a fireworks erupting from the genius of a great colourist and draughtsman, and a solid lesson of pictorial craftsmanship.

The subjects of the scenes are rather inoffensive, although the legends carry allusions and symbols of general human validity. However, from the biblical metaphors comprising parables, Tintoretto, like the other Renaissance artists, extracted the anecdotically most attractive subjects as pictorial pretexts which, whilst not contradicting the dogma in essential points, offered viewers extra-canonical and not spiritual delights. Significant as to the real relation with the ecclesiastic meaning of the subject, which has been almost totally eliminated, is the scene picturing the unexpected yet delightful erotic adventure into which the loyal and prudish Joseph is drawn by Potiphar's wife. Conciliating sensuality with piety, Tintoretto paints a beautiful nude of a great pictorial quality, chromatic value and luminosity, a model of orchestrating warm, sonorous hues in the good Venetian manner. The attitude of Potiphar's wife reminds one of the vigorous yet poetical pictures on the same subject by Giorgione and Titian. Similitude is possible, and even probable, but there is a difference between *Sleeping Venus* or *Venus of Urbino* and this carnal presence which separates deceptive, calm and self-satisfied candour from simple sensuality. The same voluptuousness of live and inanimate matter in all its concrete forms dominates the scene in which Moses is found in a basket that carries him to his destiny, actually an allegory of salvation comprising the forebodings of the future Christ cycle. The rapid brushwork, laid in a way producing a tactile transparency of each texture, homogenizes the composition so that from the pictorial viewpoint there is no difference of attitude in the interpretation of the characters, elegant Venetian women symbolizing the mythological Fates and the Graces on the one hand, and luxuriant nature, on the other, both being treated like precious brocade. From the viewpoint of substance, these two pictures do not belong to Tintoretto's best paintings, but they point to the originality of his language, the value of his associations to the art of subsequent centuries, — both Velázquez and the impressionists freely drew inspiration from this manner — and to an indubitable virtuosity of unequalled stylistic versatility.

*Susanna and the Elders*, described by Ridolfi after seeing it in the home of the painter Nicolas Régnier, was also painted in this period, probably in 1557. Resorting to suggestions outside the realm of anecdotes and enlarging the scope of analysis to include the concepts characterizing the spirit of the epoch, we rediscover a Tintoretto who is attentive and receptive to the tensions of his century. As Jacques Bousquet noted in his examination of mannerism, female nudes were obviously not discovered by the 16th. century. Novel was the sudden and constant passion for this pagan subject, surrounded by a cloudy mixture of mystery and eroticism and a diffuse polisemantic air. The classical nude is transformed into a connotative, and often coveted, presence. Its meaning is astonishingly changed, not infrequently in a cryptic direction, becoming a legitimate *concetto* of the mannerist style. Treating a non-canonical biblical subject he had already illustrated in several works, Tintoretto did not simply paint a revised reproduction, but created a new interpretation surpassing the bounds of the story itself, whose accent is on guilt and justice. This work succeeds in achieving an expressive synthesis between brilliantly displayed pictorial qualities and subtle draughtsmanship, between colour and detail, transforming it into a demonstration of virtuosity coupled

14

with a climate abounding in allusions and symbols. If the focus of observation is directed to meaning, Susanna is no longer simply a nude beautifully drawn according to the rules of new dimensions tending to lengthen the silhouette and coloured in superb Venetian hues. Full of grace and force, like a vigorous principle of vitality, Demeter and Juno, Diana and a Venetian courtesan, pointedly integrating with a décor taken from Paradise, she still embodies a nostalgic ideal of pure beauty, immune to the vice and cupidity personified by the two lewd elders. Astonishingly, the atmosphere is that of "Luxury, Calm and Voluptuousness"; Matisse recreated it nearly four centuries later with undisguised nostalgia. The scenically conceived décor in sliding planes is based on dark colours in keeping with another mannerist "trick" so that the incandescence of Susanna's body, a sensual light, detaches itself as an optic and symbolic centre. In the left part of the picture, a stag has stopped to watch the scene, in which he overemphasizes the idyllic Arcadian landscape by his emblematic presence. Dominated by mannerist tension, saturated with mysterious, cabalistic and phantastic elements, with *meraviglia*, and promoting eccentricity and the occult sciences, artists, and not only fervent practitioners like Parmigianino, manipulated cryptic symbols, among them the stag, representing the sign of alchemy for decay, for the disappearance of live matter. Interpreted in this light, and the pictorial metaphor prompts such association, the picture is not simply a gorgeous display of pictorial splendour but rather a parable of existence.

This allegory of attraction and evanescence should be considered in connexion with the phantastic, careful yet obscure scenario in the painting known as *The Liberation of Arsinoe*. Possibly the most explicitly mannerist picture of Tintoretto, which produced not only *stupore* but also a tension of restlessness, the work has an intentionally literary stance and is openly integrated with the atmosphere of the time. The subject remains ambiguous. It could illustrate two different, essentially apocryphal pretexts provided by another mannerist element, that of Alexandrine Hellenism. However, whatever the purport of the scene, its meaning does not remain at the level of a frivolous story. Its complications derive from a scheme of action dominated by fantastic features. Roger Caillois says the picture is an emblematic representation obviously designed to lead the initiated into a world of mystery, a sadic opposition between the fragility of the tempting nude and the telluric force suggested by the armour, a perverse confrontation that cannot be resolved because the physical situation is a paradox. Furthermore, mentioning other examples, meaningfully and chronologically taken from periods he calls mannerist, he emphasizes the pictorial value of the contrast between the white flesh and the dark armour serving as a screen and as a term of comparison. With this canvas, but not only with this one, Tintoretto asserts himself as an emanation and exceptional representative of the 16th. century.

At the time his new vision was taking shape, Tintoretto had already become a well-known, popular and appreciated, yet not always accepted artist, the apparent paradox being due to a natural mechanism in which curiosity and prejudice are bound to clash. Although enjoying a solid, even prosperous financial situation, he continued to work a great deal, leading the typical life of Italians having a numerous family. He was not attracted by the fashionable social life of his contemporaries, but he was a party to sterile disputes and quarrels that pretended to be about aesthetics. The complications of family life and its difficulties did not interrupt his work. Tintoretto was one of those artists whom, paraphrasing Hokusai, we may call "crazy about painting," inextricably committed to a permanent contest with the brief space of human existence and its physical limits. Like all the masters of his time, Tintoretto also worked with collaborators, among them his three gifted children, possibly the painter Domenico Molin (or Molino), his assistants Andrea Vicentino and Alberto d'Olanda, and the Greek Vasilachis, surnamed Aliense. But except for some paintings done by them with Tintoretto, the artist's work is made up of a huge number of original pieces bearing the unmistakable imprint of his personality, pictures probably ranking him first in the difficult field of big compositions for all time. Having adopted the "large manner", Tintoretto painted only few small canvases, most of them being portraits. His preference for big surfaces reflected his organic need for space and movement, and satisfied his instinct for large gestures, whose interior tension he rendered with a rapid and vigorous touch in a very modern way.

Having become famous, Tintoretto became one of the artists who were commissioned to make pictures for confraternities, churches, private persons and high Venetian officials. The Council of Ten placed quite a few orders with him for works celebrating the history of the city but also their own conceited persons. In his battle with time and the infinite temptations of art, Tintoretto made a huge number of compositions, often in the grip of dissatisfaction with himself, but always discovering new secrets in the realm of man's great spiritual adventures.

In 1562, the philosopher-doctor Tommaso Rangone of Ravenna and Grand Guardian of the Scuola Grande di San Marco, ordered, at his own expense, "three paintings with the miracles of our most holy protector and master, St. Mark." The commission was given to Tintoretto. The canvases were completed in 1566. Vasari saw them during his visit to Venice and gave an enthusiastic and quite exact description of them.

The first painting — *The Translation of the Body of St. Mark* — depicts the moment when, profiting by a storm let loose by divine forces, the Christians of Alexandria carry off the corpse of the Saint from the stake to place it in a crypt. Seen with the eyes of our present visual culture, the work is an agglomeration of plastic premonitions and premises which have asserted themselves with total autonomy in our own century. Any of the surrealists operating with the magic of anxious and mysterious exacerbated figurative art would unreservedly underwrite this fantastic composition, possibly with a feeling of wounded pride that he had not painted it himself, just as the admirers of *pittura metafisica* and of Chirico's work would feel vaguely frustrated by the unreal, terrifying, though seemingly logical architecture. Ectoplasmatic, translucid and fluid figures are rushing to the margin of the composition, driven by a terror ravaging their hearts and not by the raging storm; the centre is empty, drawing attention to the depth of the space inspired by Sansovino's scenes. On the right, forming a vigorous diagonal line accentuated by the Saint's athletic body, the group of Christians breathes a compact, concrete material nature that leaves no room for mystic implications. The tonal dominant emphasizes the dramatic character of the scene, and the red, apocalyptic sky has its counterpart in the clothing of the old man representing Tommaso Rangone. The anatomic representation and the foreshortening of the body are done in the style of Michelangelo's titanism, the gestures of the Christians are vigorous, yet restrained, and behind them, near a puzzling camel, we see Tintoretto's face to remind us of his human commitment.

Next, outlining the plot which is true to the legend of Venice's protector, the canvas titled *The Finding of the Body of St. Mark* depicts the scene in which two Venetian merchants, Buono da Malamocco and Rustico da Torcello, take the body of the Saint to convey it to their city. Here again the atmosphere is clearly mannerist, and fantastic, surrealist elements once more set their mark on a carefully arranged scene. A spectral apparition designed to emphasize the idea of spiritual immortality and ubiquity, the central character is represented in three hypostases, the one on the left dominating and structuring the scene with the authoritarian "Tintoretto gesture" which has been interpreted in various ways. Some believe it is made to prevent the profanation of the sarcophagus, a theory in contradiction with the text of the legend and also with the sequence of events. Others, among them Louis Réau, take it as a counsel intended to help the two Venetians in their task. The subtle lighting introduces a coefficient of tension akin to anxiety: the *meraviglia* is performed under our very eyes. The protagonists of the scene, including the old man, probably also representing Rangone, overwhelmed by the miracle, stand out as in a play, while the opening, placed at the end of an absorbing perspective, seems to be the only solution feasible in this metaphysical equation: return to the light. Movement is accelerated, the motion is disharmonious and centrifugal, and incipient Baroque thinking is discernible in the midst of the wealth of mannerist artifice.

The last piece of the series — *St. Mark Rescuing a Saracen from Shipwreck* — is done in the mannerist spirit and abounds in its favourite signs: a sulphurous, apocalyptic sky, subtly elongated, vigorous figures, an agitated sea, and the theatrical intervention of the Saint rescuing the converted heathen. As expected, Tommaso Rangone is in this picture as well, this time in a vigorous posture, and the throbbing scene, with dispersed angles and a dilated anatomic tumult, appears more strongly oriented towards the as yet unestablished Baroque spirit.

Summing up the contradictory feelings produced by the three paintings and seeking to sum them up in their spirit, we shall have to accept the fact — and the material needed for comparison and meditation, if not for persuasion is now furnished by time — that Tintoretto was a great forerunner.

The year 1564 gave the artist his unique opportunity of making his definitive and triumphant entry in history, like Michelangelo some thirty years before him, and he did so with the significantly named "Venetian Sistine."

The youngest philantropic religious fraternity, called Scuola Grande di San Rocco, had a rapid development, despite the unimpressive biography of its recently sanctified patron. Already flourishing as a typical Venetian institution in the 13th. century, it was recognized by the Council of Ten on 10th. June 1478. In 1535, when its headquarters was completed, the council of the brotherhood began to consider how its rooms should be decorated. Titian's suggestions, set out in a letter he wrote in 1553, were never carried out. Discussions were resumed in 1564, and it was decided that a competition be held for the commission.

It was a hotly debated event at the time, and its echoes were still clearly audible when Vasari arrived at Venice in 1566. The well-informed and passionate biographer Ridolfi gives an attractive, and sometimes thrilling account of all the details. Here are the main points of his story. After the brotherhood announced the competition, Paolo Veronese, Andrea Schiavone, Giuseppe Salviati, Federico Zuccaro and Tintoretto decided to participate in it. The latter *secretamente* procured the measurements of the ceiling of the Sala dell'Albergo where *The Glorification of St. Roch* was to be placed and in keeping with his custom, which produced stupefaction and even protest, painted the canvas in oil, without any preparatory sketches or drawings. On the appointed day, the other competitors presented their plans and Tintoretto the finished picture, which *artificiosamente aveva ottorato con un cartone.* His opponents unanimously proclaimed the deserved victory of the most gifted and rapid entrant, an attitude to be expected in a fashionable novel of morals, and the artist declared he offered the painting as a free gift in homage of St. Roch. This fine story throws a favourable light on loyal and generous competitors and great credit on Tintoretto. As a matter of fact, though, there was quite a considerable opposition to the artist. One of the Council members, Mario Zuan Zignioni, offered to pay 15 ducats if the commission went to another painter. However, Tintoretto had made a cool calculation. He knew that according to the rules of the brotherhood his gift could not be refused, and being accepted, he would have a moral advantage when the commission was adjudicated. And he proved to be right.

On 22nd. June 1564, the council decided by 31 votes to 22 that the commission be given to Tintoretto.

The master and prisoner of several hundred square metres that had to be covered by paintings, facing an amount of work that would have intimidated any other artist, but resolved to do the job, Tintoretto set out with that "furious elan" which generated a new style. And his gifted, feverish hand produced a message of so far unprecedented human dimensions.

There was an idea, which gradually became a prejudice, according to which Tintoretto was a great mystic. He certainly was a believer, although in a particular way we would now call Venetian. Certainly not a bigot, he was not an atheist. The scenes he pictured for a brotherhood had to be canonic, but their real content, their implicit meaning, the feelings of drama and glory, of tragedy and triumph were not those of the Church; they were those of Man, the creator of his own divinity.

Tintoretto has also been called an artisan of the Baroque style, meaning a new compositional, anatomic and luministic concept dominated by spatial dynamic. However, at the time of its peak, in the 17th. century, the Baroque signified, beyond its specific formal and eventually recurrent structure, which is typical of every constant element, a certain essentially and even excessive religious attitude born of the Catholic spirit that had been sharpened by its clash with the Reformation. An attitude alien to Tintoretto, who was much too engrossed with the working out of a new plastic philosophy deriving from modified 16th. century humanism to lose himself in the labyrinth of sterile mystic speculations. "In Tintoretto's painting," writes Moschini, "the Christian myths have a new, unreal, transfigured look, and a visionary accent that introduces something absolutely new in our art." And Pallucchini, minutely examining all the implications of the great Venetian, says: "This impetuous dramatic concept, together with unbounded phantasy, gathered into so coherent a form make Tintoretto one of the artists who are very close to modern sensibility." This point of view has to be remembered when considering the whole work of Tintoretto, and especially when looking at the paintings at the Scuola di San Rocco.

Entirely done by the artist himself, from a perspective that excluded any intervention on the part of anyone not identifying with the spirit and meaning of this unique masterpiece, the Venetian Sistine offered Tintoretto not only "the means of clearly and unequivocally leaving the mark of his genius," as Pallucchini put it, but also of conveying the message of a man receptive to all the contradictions and changes of his time to his contemporaries and posterity.

When he shouldered his difficult and impassioned task with heroic daring, Tintoretto knew that his own views would have to resist and actually dominate the inherent canonic obligations. That is why he reserved the right, within the rather unclear limits of the envisaged pictorial programe, to give the scenes his own interpretation, lending them emotional and symbolic meanings he himself had discovered behind the screen of so far conventionally treated events and legends.

The first project of the huge decoration, the Sala dell'Albergo, completed in 1566, had 23 works on the ceiling and walls. Tintoretto's solution was typical of his style: oils on canvas fixed in the places chosen for each scene, a procedure enabling him to work rapidly and using brilliant chromatics for the vigorous definition of the characters and of physical space. The grand design is revealed by the Christ cycle, in which Charles de Tolnay detects the metaphoric meaning of the artist's concept. The key to it is given by the portraits of two prophets looking at the main pieces of the composition: one in the direction of *Christ before Pilate*, *Ecce Homo* and *Christ on the Way to Calvary*, and the others at the *Crucifixion*, a hallucinating scene, in which a crowd overwhelmed by tragedy is drawn into tumultuous movement. Its compositional and pictorial effects, as well as its size, make this the probably most impressive piece. This huge pictorial poem represents the most complex and most daring attempt to depict the whole wide range of sentiment, reaction and attitude produced by the crucifixion. Taking each emotional, dramatic, spiritual and human implication and analysing the closely-knit, novel and yet logical, concept that nevertheless remains subject to different interpretations, one might write a screen-play in which the cross-current of ideas and their mutual enrichment can correspond to the painting itself. Pallucchini sees the *Crucifixion* as "a brilliant example of composition of all time and not only of Venetian art," and ascribes its quality to the inextricable logic in the distribution of the light and of the lines of force. The body of Christ crucified, a body of very human physical force, becomes the centre of the painting. Around him revolve the crowd, grouped as in a carefully prepared script: soldiers, executioners, spectators and, at the foot of the cross, the three Marys with Nicodemus and John embodying an image of sorrow and despair. The material perspective, emphasized by the grave, despondent colouring and the surrealistic, convulsive characters in the background, strains towards the infinite. The symbolic and emotional perspective advances towards the viewer, due to the placing of the crowd along two diagonals that meet at the foot of the cross. The sky is dramatic, forecasting a storm. An unreal light seems to issue from the body of Christ. The scene is replete with mystery and tension at the point of breaking equilibrium, and with an as yet undefined anxiety. This is a highly mannerist atmosphere, but the profound feeling and the physical weight of the participants in the scene exclude any intention of escaping into the zone of gratuitously spectacular effects just to produce stupefaction. The left side of the background is dominated by an ambiguous obelisk of unexplained significance. The group of phantomatic armoured horsemen in the foreground looks like an allegory of implacable force. Before long, it reappeared, essentially the same, in the work of another hallucinating genius, Tintoretto's disciple El Greco. The *Crucifixion* was painted in the year Tintoretto was admitted to the brotherhood, by 85 votes for and 19 against. It is dated and signed: MDLXV TEMPORE MAGNIFICI DOMINI HIERONIMI ROTAE ET COLLEGARUM IACOBUS TINTORETUS FACIEBAT.

The following year, 1566, Tintoretto completed the decoration of the Sala dell'Albergo and, in recognition of his talent and repute, was invited to join the Florentine Academy with Palladio, Salviati and Titian. In the ten years that passed before he resumed the decoration of the Scuola di San Rocco, Tintoretto's art acquired an even more authoritarian tone of its own, a mixture of declared realism and phantasy. Its luministic formula is a succession of variations on solutions based on chiaroscuro. One of the landmarks in this evolution is the *Last Supper* painted for San Trovaso in Venice, a model in a cycle he constantly returned to, and re-interpreted from, the emotional and pictorial viewpoints. The composition lives by the great originality of the arrangement of the characters, by its popular air, later also found with Caravaggio, by the realistic portraits, some of which are almost brutal, and the anything but mystical atmosphere of the scene, looking more like the libation of workmen than a religious gathering. Paying his usual attention to the symbol value of light and its pictorial trait, Tintoretto places Christ against the background of the only opening on the outside, thus obtaining an effect of great tension. The diaphanous figures outside the building, between the columns, have something unreal about them in their apparently virtual levitation. An old woman, oblivious to everything, spinning in the obscurity of the flight of stairs so dear to Tintoretto, but also to Rembrandt, seems to impersonate fate implacably twisting its thread, a pagan mythological allegory organically introduced in a Christian canonic representation.

Among the numerous works of this period, there is a *Self-portrait* done for the Scuola di San Rocco. The inscription and date, RELIGIONI/1573, have been interpreted in various ways. Hadeln believes the picture is a portrait of a member of the brotherhood, while Pallucchini considers it as a small *ex-voto* representing the human creator of these masterpieces.

In a different tone, in the spirit of the great mythological allegories, painted with an undisguised joy of returning to a golden age lacking strain and tension, vaguely libertine and yet pervaded by a classical purity, the four canvases for the Palazzo Ducale represent an interesting and attractive chapter. Executed, according to their assessment by Paolo Veronese and Palma the Younger, about 1576, these pictures are an *a priori* entity both from the viewpoint of concept and of their dominant metaphors. Charles de Tolnay has interpreted them as an allegory of the four seasons, as a cosmological rounding out of the allegory dedicated to the rule of Doge Girolamo Priuli. *Mercury and the Graces* is commented upon by Ridolfi from the angle of mythological meaning, and also in the context of the fate of Venice. Tolnay sees in it the representation of spring and of air. Ridolfi explains the scene with *Bacchus, with Ariadne crowned by Venus* in the spirit of the legend, but also views it as an allegory of Venice, seated on the seashore and crowned with the laurels of liberty. Here again, Tolnay adds an essential element, discovering in the gesture of Bacchus, who offers his ring, the symbol of Venice's betrothal to the sea, and also an allegory of autumn and water. According to Ridolfi, *Pallas Athene and Mars* represents the triumph of concord secured by the wisdom of Venice, so that peace and abundance may thrive in peace, and according to Tolnay the canvas also pictures an allegory of summer and earth, the vital source. *The Forge of Vulcan* is said to represent the unity of action of all Venetian senators in strengthening the city's military power; Tolnay sees an allegory of winter — in the snow-covered landscape — and of fire. Hence we have two interpretations — separated by three centuries — which actually do not contradict one another. One spotlights the mythological meaning, the other, modern and subtle, discovers a new, literary and more "mannerist" angle. However, both highlight the complex nature of Tintoretto's art, its polisemantics and affective symbols, all of them served by a pictorial mastery which in and by itself would be sufficient to make these works valuable.

Nevertheless, the decoration of the premises of the confraternity to which he now belonged, remained, if not the only, his principal preoccupation. His passion and interest were focused on it. In 1575 he offered to execute, free of charge, a ceiling painting representing the biblical legend of *The Erection of the Brazen Serpent* in the large upper hall of the Scuola di San Rocco. Completed in 1576, it was followed, after quite a few discussions, by large-size paintings for the ceiling and the walls, gradually adding up to an original vision of unique spiritual and pictorial significance. The cycle of pictures illustrates biblical subjects selected for their profoundly human meaning: man's salvation from moral and physical disease.

The alternating episodes explain one another. The prophetic meaning of certain episodes from the Old Testament explicitly asserts itself on the scale of general human values through the cycles from the New Testament, thus producing what has been called *Concordia Veteris et Novi Testamenti*. Intuiting the intended parallelism of the subjects in the Sala grande superiore, their message conceived in a single cycle, Thode advances the hypothesis of a rigorous programme initially drawn up by some learned members of the brotherhood. The studies made by other researchers, though, resumed and summed up by Charles de Tolnay, demonstrate that the entire "dramaturgy" was detailed scene after scene in succession and as each subject demanded new interpretations and additions. Such was the genesis of the nucleus deserving the name of Venetian Sixtine, still astonishing as an ensemble and often stupendous in its diverse parts. Never before, says Tolnay, had the artist employed light with a more "scenographic" intelligence and ability, thereby transforming the semi-darkness of the hall into an active pictorial factor required for the entire composition of space. In this pathetic agglomeration of Christian scenes, symbols and mysteries, the three dominant themes — salvation from sickness, hunger and thirst — are represented as an existential parable. In this analysis and interpretation, the unitary decoration reveals its real meaning, its homogeneous essence deriving from subordination to an all-pervading principle.

The first episode of the Christ cycle, in chronological order, is *The Nativity*, or *Adoration of the Shepherds*, and it seems to have astonished Tintoretto's contemporaries. Renouncing the traditional scheme, as he had on other occasions, the artist took the liberty of separating the scene into two horizontal registers, thereby strikingly suggesting the difference between the miracle and the concrete, real world. The Holy Virgin and Child, and Joseph, are placed in the loft of the stable, and assisted by angels looking down from the clouds, while the shepherds and traditional animals — the ox and the ass — are grouped in and around the manger. An unreal light comes from somewhere far above, and it falls in a way producing theatrical effects. The centre of the scene is free. The viewer's attention involuntarily descends towards two figures having definite iconographic functions: the peacock, formerly the pagan symbol of Juno and now of the Child's eternity, and the cock who banishes the night, but also heralds the betrayal of Peter and, at the other pole of existence, the resurrection. Still unusual to viewers today due to its composition and special tone, the scene must have looked almost blasphemous to the artist's contemporaries. Writing half a century after its completion, Ridolfi called it an extravagant invention. The scene acquires a new sense of magic lyricism and, as Pallucchini put it, ". . . only Rembrandt knew how to address himself to men in such a way."

*The Baptism of Christ* carries forward the lyrical values of the preceding scene on a different plane, and it adds an amplified, modern element of phantasy. The elaborate composition is dynamized by the horizontal water and vertical mountain in the foreground, despite the immobility of the characters pictured in the symbolic act. The strange light on the protagonists comes from a mannerist sky. The forms of the other characters, painted with a convulsive, decisive touch, are transparent and immaterial. Once again, the *meraviglia* puts its mark on the inner meaning of the scene. Emotional tension appears to have reached a climax. Obsession with revelation justifies the entire atmosphere. Once again, Tintoretto is a visionary of the spirit. The symbolical purification proceeds on a high moral and psychological level. Man finds himself.

The same metaphorical intentions govern the agitated personages in *The Last Supper*, one of the works marking a new stage in the artist's thinking and style. The Renaissance model has been left far behind. The *teoria* of the companions, formerly seated parallel to the viewer, is destroyed by the breath of uneasiness disturbing the apostles, actually the breath that also displayed the certitudes postulated up to the 16th. century. The restlessness produced by the thought of treason, incompatible with the generous concept of brotherhood and mutual trust that reigned between them so far as a human principle, now put its stamp on them. The scene has something of a still. It has something "pre-cinematographic." The diagonal line of the table allows for a new and very modern emphasis: although the smallest figure, Christ, seated at the extremity of a symbolical perspective, monopolizes the attention, the other companions have the same, somewhat pathetic but vigorous, human air. Their movements animate the several planes of the composition. The background is a separate universe, isolated from the drama taking its course in the centre of the room, like the foreground, where we see several persons in their everyday pursuits, and a dog.

The presence of these characters is motivated by the philanthropic nature of the Scuola and the attributes of San Rocco, and the artist succeeds in the simultaneous rendering of an explicit allegory and a fine still life, with fruit and vases, which tends to assert a plastic autonomy. Here again, a flight of stairs enters the expressive pictorial composition as a compositional and symbolic element. The big space is deployed for affective purposes, exploiting the antinomy between the first room, lighted by two sources, and the small rooms which lend themselves to an interpretation in the style of genre scenes definitely established by the artists of the Netherlands whose works must have been known to and appreciated by Tintoretto.

Described by Bercken-Mayer as "one of the most impetuous and visionary scenes of the cycle painted at San Rocco," *The Ascension* also strikingly separates the two planes of existence, without diminishing the inner unity of the composition, the common denominator of transfigured humanity. Celestial glory is based on classical attributes, angels with fan-shaped espaliers and olive leaves. The whole procession is projected into space with a manifest force, also involving the conventional element of clouds, having a broiling density, whilst the apostles witnessing the miracle, incapable of continuing their intended movements, look like being hypnotized. The character in the foreground becomes one of the sliding planes through which the accelerated perspective emphasizes an accentuated compositional depth, while the swiftly sketched outlines remain in the ambiguous zone of immaterial, or at least incorporeal beings, a sensation that is amplified by the tonal dialogue. And once again, the light, that co-worker and director of the scenes painted by Tintoretto, produces that particular, irradiant and unreal note typical of his personal interpretations of symbols.

The final chapter in the decoration of the confraternity's premises was written in the years 1583—1587, at a time when the artist, tortured by a turmoil of doubt, reach the apex of passionate inventiveness and pictorial autonomy. The *Sala terrena* reaffirms his determination to group images round a single, unitarian nucleus that launches an explicit rendering of the life of the Virgin and of Christ in six large canvases. Two rather "romantic" works, *St. Mary of Egypt* and *St. Mary Magdalen* evince the artist's intention to expand the area of general existential implications. As noted by Tolnay, Tintoretto gave the entire cycle a popular tone, altogether different from the traditional ecclesiastic pomp and close to the concept of a *Biblia pauperum* accessible to all. The biblical subject becomes an up to a point credible human experience. A genre scene reveals a miracle. The dominant feature is not canonical. That is why several commentators have put forward the theory of a certain contact with the ideas of the Reformation, which Tintoretto must have known, without, however, accepting its dogma. Moreover, certain pictorial elements, particularly his unusual treatment of the landscape, have given currency to the view that he was influenced by Dürer, known in Italy especially for his engravings, and by the Danubian school which had introduced into European art an interpretation of nature in a "pre-romantic," large, dramatic and even anxious spirit that claimed the right to an autonomous esthetic existence. These attractive theories, which we can only briefly mention in this brief outline, could be the subject of an entire literature.

The decoration of the *Sala terrena* comprises a great deal of originality, passion and pictorial expressiveness. *The Annunciation* impresses by its profane character and the clearly symbolic scenographic idea based on the surprise produced by the appearance of the group of angels in their dizzy dive. *The Flight into Egypt* most certainly dominates the entire cycle with its human and visionary force. The composition exploits the difference between the group, intentionally representing the Holy Family in a very terrestrial stance, and the peculiar, unquiet landscape — according to Clark a drama of light and shadow as impressive as with Altdorfer — which is the setting of customary pursuits. Much has been said about the group of three, placed in a light that seems to issue from the bodies of the characters, and about the elements in the still life in the foreground, so minute as to suggest the fetishism typical of art in the Netherlands or, according to Pallucchini, recalling the work of the Venetian painter Carpaccio. All these references and cross references as to possible and probable influences show that Tintoretto was, as he obviously had to be, aware of all artistic achievements in Europe and, at the same time, a singular continuer of a unique experience crystallized in Italian art. The forceful expression and symbolized tonal relation between the red garment of Joseph and the blue mantle of Mary, which become the optical centre of the picture, again reminds us of the persistence of Venetian tradition. Altogether different as to the subject matter, though similar as to attitude, *St. Mary of Egypt* is placed, contrary to tradition, not in a desert, but near a forest of the Northern, romantic kind, with a mysterious, hallucinating atmosphere, worthy of Caspar David Friedrich or Josef Anton Koch, by which the artist integrates his own passionate feeling in the flux of nature. We suddenly realize that the tone has changed, and also see the concrete pictorial quality for which the romantics admired their Mediterranean forerunner who had found the means of introducing human beings into the landscape with the feeling of consubstantiality.

Less impressive as to content and tension, *The Adoration of the Magi* is a chromatically well balanced picture, an asymmetrical composition in which the principal group is advancing in the foreground although the most stirring element is the procession on the right, a cavalcade of fantastic beings Tintoretto felt he had to place there to complete the decoration of the Sala terrena.

Still vigorous, but paying much more attention to the inner tone of the ideas he depicted, and reflecting, not without a certain bitterness and resignation, on the meaning of human existence, Tintoretto now produced fewer works by himself, resorted to the assistance of his co-workers and concentrated on particularly interesting paintings that became landmarks of his last period. However, even the pictures done by his co-workers evince his artistic intelligence and unifying force. Nevertheless, between the enormous *Paradise*, now considered by experts as a workshop piece, and the oil model in the Louvre, of a dynamic spontaneity only equalled by its chromatic brilliance, there is a difference that separates the expressive power of genius from the correct application of a difficult lesson learned by disciples who possess no more than capable hands. This attempt to render celestial glory in a novel way poses interesting problems of iconography and composition involving, in the main, passionate and absorbing concepts and formulae of a profane philosophical essence. The painting pictures the whole train of sacred personages in a rigorous hierarchical order, placed concentrically round a mysterious nucleus, a plasmatic centre giving forth human beings. The composition is dynamic, the figures have very different positions, being drawn into a centripetal movement. And, as with Michelangelo, anatomies of the most authentic earthly corporeal nature populate an unreal space with their palpable presence. The quick, vigorous brushwork used to depict most of the secondary characters, dissolves in the atmosphere of an almost touchable tension. The concentric ellipses appear to reconstrue the order described by Dante. Their tone is poetic and visionary but, as Hocke has suggested, they could also be a pictorial interpretation of new scientific truths which sounded altogether unlikely and paradoxical in Tintoretto's contradictory century. In 1543, Copernicus had published his capital *De revolutionibus orbium celestium, libri IV*, and with its publication the earth had ceased being the centre of the universe. And in 1583—1584 Giordano Bruno had published his famous works which condemned him in the eyes of his narrow-minded and prejudiced contemporaries (cf. Chronology). At least three years before Tintoretto painted his *Paradise*, Bruno declared that every circular movement must change its trajectory into an ellipse straining toward the infinite, like the celestial grouping in the artist's picture. Believing that this might be more than a simple coincidence, and viewing the painting from our own century, we can separate the religious meaning of the immediate imagery from the parable of existence and apotheosis of man in one of the most daring, and probably as yet unequalled, symbolic compositions.

And now we come to the last grandiose vision in the long life of a visionary attracted only by the grandeur of the spirit and of art. His old and permanent obsession with the subject materializes in a monumental and phantastic *Last Supper* in the presbytery of San Giorgio Maggiore, a veritable recital of chiaroscuro and the summing up of experiments done over a period of more than fifty years, to which the great Venetian painter, artist and philosopher, dedicated to matter and spirit, had linked his whole life. Reality is embodied in human beings and fascinating details of still lives distributed in space as autonomous units. The atmosphere has an air of irreality. Ectoplasmatic figures fill the room as in a dream foreshadowing the spiritual drama of the apostles, freezing them in symbolical attitudes which, as in Leonardo da Vinci's masterpiece, could represent the twelve months of the year. Unaware of the mystery they are witnessing, the secondary characters are moving with a restrained force and elegance, typical of Tintoretto, in a ritual of domestic chores involving the Venetian pomp of ordinary objects, in striking contrast with the emotional and transcendent nature of the scene. The focus of the drama shifts to the left side of the painting. The diagonal formed by the table organizes the entire composition in an unusual perspective. Due to the theatrical lighting, the "Tintoretto effect" becomes even more explicit. The suspended lamp and Christ are the centres of confrontation between the spiritual and the material quality of light. In this atmosphere, abounding in surrealistic signs and symbols, and comprising spectral apparitions, pictorial effects and elements producing astonishment to this day. The tonal orchestration is based on two basic chords, red and blue, modulated in subtle chromatic variants and linked to a purposeful inner symbolism. Matter becomes precious. A tactile feeling lends every object a material concreteness as in the paintings of the Flemish school. The setting is construed with great sophistication, despite the apparent disorder in the room. The dominant emotional feeling reaches the intensity of the most striking experiences of modern life, which makes the term "expressionism" Pallucchini used to describe the climate of the work, fully appropriate.

After completing his cycle of Last Suppers painted throughout his career with this *Last Supper* in the presbytery of San Giorgio Maggiore, Tintoretto, "by the grace of God healthy in spirit and mind, but with a sick body," made his last will on 30th. March 1594. Having accumulated a huge human and artistic experience, Tintoretto left everything he had to his son Domenico, asking him to share everything, and particularly his artistic experience, with his brother Marco. It was a will worthy of a unique artist.

The "magnificent Jacopo di Robusti, also called Tintoretto, died at the age of 75 years and 8 months, after 15 days of fever, in the parish of San Marcilio." The body sheltering the most restless spirit of a restless century, the receptacle of "the most terrific brains of art" was buried in the Santa Maria dell'Orto, watched by the paintings he had made in that modest church, below the symbolic stairs of *The Presentation in the Temple* which he had ascended to reach the peaks of his vocation.

# CHRONOLOGY
# AND CONCORDANCES

1518    Birth of Jacopo Robusti, son of the dyer Giovanni Battista Robusti, from Lucca, at the end of September or early October. A brother, Domenico, lives at Mantua.

1519    *Michelangelo starts decorating the Medici Chapel.*
1520    *Jacopo Pontormo paints the frescoes for the Medici Villa.*
         *Luther burns the papal edict of admonestation and is excommunicated.*
1521—1526. *The first war between François I and Charles V for the possession of Italy.*
1523    *Parmigianino paints his famous mannerist* Selfportrait.
1526—1529. *The second war between François I and Charles V, after which France gives up its claims to Italy.*
1527    *Sacco di Roma, the sacking of the city and destruction of property by the soldiers of Charles V.*
1527    *Restoration of the Florentine Republic. The Medicis are expelled from the city.*
1528    *Birth of Paolo Caliari, Veronese.*
         *Death of Albrecht Dürer (b. 1471).*
1529    *Under the terms of the Paix des Dames concluded at Cambrai, Venice loses Ravenna and the Apulian towns.*
1532    *Publication of Macchiavelli's* Il Principe.
1534    *Ignatius de Loyola founds the Society of Jesus, or Order of Jesuits, recognized by the Pope in 1540. Michelangelo makes his first cardboards for the wall paintings in the Sixtine Chapel, which he completed in 1541.*
1536    *Jacopo Sansovino starts work on the San Marco Library in Venice.*

1539    The first document mentioning Tintoretto. It is a will, which he signs "Jo mistro Giacomo depentor."
1540    Tintoretto's first signed picture, *Sacra conversazione.* The name Jacobus is followed by a wheel. Von Hadeln believed it was done by the painter Molin, whose real name was Domenico. Carlo Bernari thinks the wheel represents the sign of the dyers' guild, who use a wheel to stretch cloth, hence the signature should read: Jacobus, the dyer's son.

1541    *Birth of Domeniko Theotocopoulos, El Greco, at Fodela on Crete. The great painter was strongly influenced by Tintoretto.*

1545    Pietro Aretino writes to Tintoretto praising him and thanking him for his two ceiling paintings.

1545—1563 *The Council of Trent elaborates the doctrine and strategy of the Counter-Reformation.*
1550    *Giorgio Vasari published the first edition of his Biographies.*

         Tintoretto marries Faustina Episcopi (dei Vescovi), daughter of the Grand Guardian of the Scuola Grande di San Marco.
1556    Birth of Tintoretto's daughter Marietta. She became a painter.

1559    *Treaty of Cateau-Cambrésis. Italy remains under Spanish domination. End of the Italic Wars.*

1560    Birth of Tintoretto's second son, Domenico, who became a painter. The birth date of his first son, Giovanni Battista, is not known.
1561    Birth of Marco, Tintoretto's third son, also a painter.
1562    Birth of Tintoretto's second daughter Perina. She became a nun.

1563    *Veronese paints his famous* Marriage at Cana *which inaugurated a new style in Venetian painting.*

1564    Tintoretto starts decorating the Sala dell'Albergo of the Scuola di San Rocco.
1565    Tintoretto becomes a member of the San Rocco confraternity.
1566    Together with Titian, Salviati and Palladio, Tintoretto becomes a member of the Florentine Academy.

         *Palladio starts work on the church of San Giorgio Maggiore at Venice.*

1570    Birth of Tintoretto's daughter Ottavia. She would later take the veil.

1571 *The battle of Lepanto. The Christian fleet under the command of Don Juan of Austria defeats the Turks.*

1573 *Birth of Michelangelo Merisi da Caravaggio, who launched a new trend in realism, based on chiaroscuro, which had a strong impact on European art.*

1576 Tintoretto starts decorating the Big Hall of the Scuola di San Rocco.

1577 *Birth of Peter Paul Rubens, the master of Baroque.*

1580 *Tintoretto travels to Mantua to supervise the positioning of the canvases of the* Gonzaga Fasti.

   Probable birth year of Franz Hals, one of the world's great portrait painters.

1581 Tintoretto completes the decoration of the Big Hall.

1583 Tintoretto starts work on the paintings for the Lower Hall in the Scuola di San Rocco.

1583—1584 *Giordano Bruno publishes his* Cena de la Ceneri; Della Causa, Principio, ed Uno, *and* Del' Infinito, Universo, e Mondi.

1585 Birth of Tintoretto's daughter Lanza. The birth date of his fifth daughter, Altura, is not known.

1587 Tintoretto finishes the decoration of the Lower Hall.

1590 Death of Marietta, a loss that strongly accentuated Tintoretto's depressive mood.

1592 Tintoretto is elected to the Scuola dei Mercanti.

1594 Jacopo Robusti Tintoretto dies on May 31st.

# SELECTED BIBLIOGRAPHY

GIORGIO VASARI, *Le Vite*, Milanesi, Firenza, 1881

HEINRICH THODE, *Tintoretto*, Bielefeld-Leipzig, 1901.

RODOLFO PALLUCCHINI, *Tintoretto a San Rocco, Le tre Venezie*, Venice, 1937.

PIETRO ARETINO, *Lettere*, Ortolani, Torino, 1945.

HANS TIETZE, *Tintoretto, Gemälde und Zeichnungen*, London, 1948.

HEINRICH WÖLFFLIN, *Principes fondamentaux de l'histoire de l'art*, Gallimard, 1952.

LIONELLO VENTURI, *De Leonard au Greco*, Skira, Genève, 1956.

GIUSEPPE DE LOGU, *Pittura veneziana*, Istituto Italiano d'Arte Grafiche, Bergamo, 1958.

GIULIANO BRIGANTI, *Le Maniérisme italien*, VEB Edition, Leipzig, 1962.

JACQUES BOUSQUET, *La peinture maniériste*, Ides et Calendes, Neuchâtel, 1964.

RENÉ HUYGHE, *Les puissances de l'image*, Flammarion, Paris, 1965.

ANDREI OȚETEA, *Renașterea și Reforma* (Renaissance and Reformation), Ed. Științifică, Bucharest, 1968.

ANDRÉ CHASTEL, *La crise de la Renaissance*, Skira, Genève, 1968.

FRED BÉRANCE, *La Renaissance italienne*, B. Arthaud, Paris, 1966.

FREDERICK HARTT, *A History of Italian Renaissance Art*, Thames and Hudson, London, 1970.

ROGER CAILLOIS, *Au coeur du fantastique*, Ed. Gallimard, Paris, 1965.

*\*\* Tout l'oeuvre peint de Tintoret*, Flammarion, Paris, 1971.

BERNARD BERENSON, *The Italian Painters of the Renaissance*, Oxford University Press, London, 1966.

GUSTAV RENÉ HOCKE, *Die Welt als Labyrinth*, Rowohlt Taschenbuch Verlag GmbH, Hamburg, 1957

# LIST OF ILLUSTRATIONS

27. CHRIST ON THE WAY TO CALVARY
1566—1567
5.15×3.80 m.
oils on canvas
Scuola di San Rocco, Venice

28. THE ERECTION OF THE BRAZEN
SERPENT
1575—1576
8.40×5.20 m.
oils on canvas
Scuola di San Rocco, Venice

29. SELF-PORTRAIT
1573
0.72×0.57 m.
oils on canvas
Scuola di San Rocco, Venice

30. CHRIST IN THE HOUSE OF
MARTHA AND MARY
1567
1.975×1.31 m.
oils on canvas
Alte Pinakothek, München

31. THE LAST SUPPER
1566
2.21×4.13 m.
oils on canvas
San Trovaso, Venice

32. CHRIST IN THE HOUSE OF
MARTHA AND MARY (detail from 30)

33. THE FORGE OF VULCAN
1576
1.45×1.56 m.
oils on canvas
Palazzo Ducale, Venice

34. THE POOL OF BETHESDA (detail)
1579—1581
5.33×5.29 m.
oils on canvas
Scuola di San Rocco, Venice

35. CHRIST BEFORE PILATE
1566—1567
5.15×3.80 m.
oils on canvas
Scuola di San Rocco, Venice

36. THE CRUCIFIXION
1568
3.41×3.71 m.
oils on canvas
San Cassiano, Venice

37. THE ADORATION OF THE MAGI
1579—1581
5.42×4.55 m.
oils on canvas
Scuola di San Rocco, Venice

38. THE ASCENSION
1579—1581
5.38×3.25 m.
oils on canvas
Scuola di San Rocco, Venice

39. BACCHUS, WITH ARIADNE
CROWNED BY VENUS
1576
1.46×1.67 m.
oils on canvas
Palazzo Ducale, Venice

40. MERCURY AND THE THREE
GRACES
1576
1.46×1.55 m.
oils on canvas
Palazzo Ducale, Venice

41. THE GATHERING OF THE MANNA
1577
5.50×5.20 m.
oils on canvas
Scuola di San Rocco, Venice

42. THE LAST SUPPER
1579—1581
5.38×4.87 m.
oils on canvas
Scuola di San Rocco, Venice

43. FRANCESCO II GONZAGA IN THE
BATTLE OF TARO (from
THE GONZAGA FASTI cycle)
1578—1579
2.69×4.22 m.
Alte Pinakothek, München

44. PALLAS ATHENE AND MARS
1576
1.48×1.68 m.
oils on canvas
Palazzo Ducale, Venice

45. THE ORIGIN OF THE MILKY WAY
1582
1.48×1.65 m.
oils on canvas
National Gallery, London

46. THE BAPTISM OF CHRIST, detail
1579—1581
5.38×4.65 m.
oils on canvas
Scuola di San Rocco, Venice

47. THE FLIGHT INTO EGYPT, detail
1583—1587
4.22×5.80 m.
oils on canvas
Scuola di San Rocco, Venice

48. THE FLIGHT INTO EGYPT
detail

49. EZECHIEL'S DREAM
1577—1578
6.60×2.65 m.
oils on canvas
Scuola di San Rocco, Venice

50. IONA AND THE WHALE
1577—1578
2.65×3.70 m.
oils on canvas
Scuola di San Rocco, Venice

51. THE PARADISE
1588—1592
1.43×3.62 m.
oils on canvas
The Louvre, Paris

52. ST. MARY MAGDALEN
1583—1587
4.25×2.09 m.
oils on canvas
Scuola di San Rocco, Venice

53. ST. MARY OF EGYPT
1583—1587
4.25×2.11 m.
oils on canvas
Scuola di San Rocco, Venice

54. ST. MARY OF EGYPT
detail

55. THE SAMARITAN
1578
1.16×0.93 m.
oils on canvas
Uffizi, Florence

1. Allegory of Music

2. The Last Supper
3. The Last Supper (detail)

4. St. Mark Rescuing a Slave (detail)

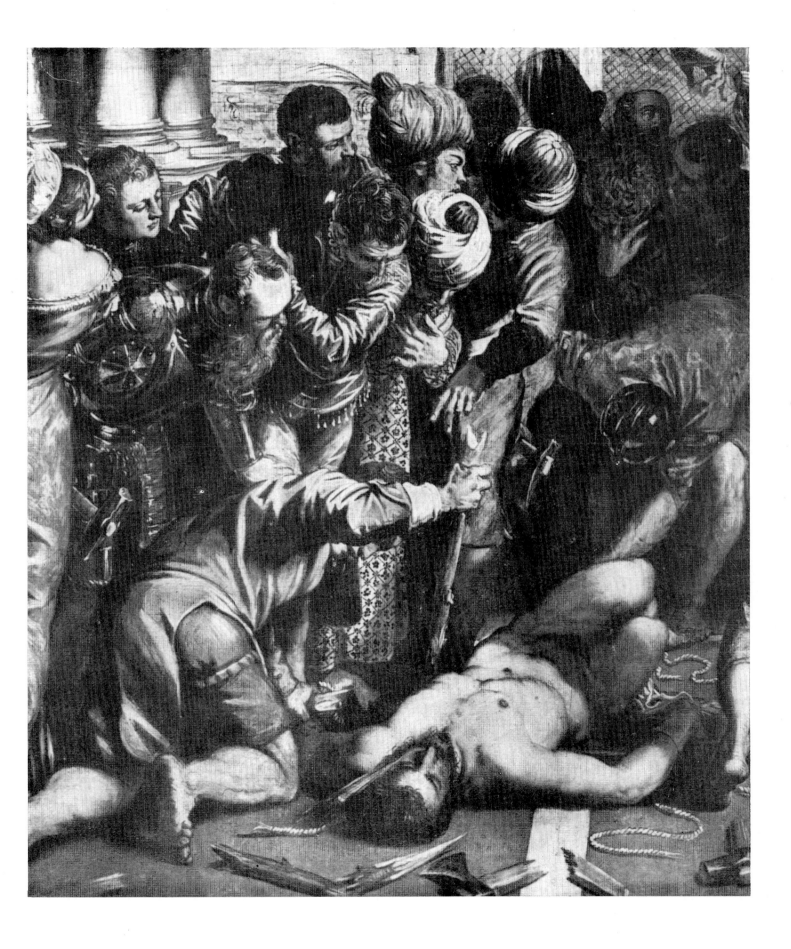

5. St. Mark Rescuing a Slave

6. Christ Washing the Feet of the Apostles
7. Presentation of the Virgin in the Temple (detail)

8. Presentation of the Virgin in the Temple (detail)

9. Presentation of the Virgin in the Temple

11. Portrait of a Woman in Black

13. Joseph and Potiphar's Wife
14. The Liberation of Arsinoe

15. Susanna and the Elders (detail)
16. Susanna and the Elders

19. The Translation of the Body of St. Mark (detail)

20. The Deposition
21. The Crucifixion (detail)

23. The Crucifixion (fragment)

25. Bearded Man with Fur (fragment)

26. Madonna and Child (fragment)

31. The Last Supper
32. Christ in the House of Martha and Mary (detail from 30)

34. The Pool of Bethesda (detail)

38. The Ascension

39. Bacchus, with Ariadne Crowned by Venus

40. Mercury and the Three Graces

42. The Last Supper

43. Francesco II Gonzaga in the Battle of Taro (detail)
44. Pallas Athene and Mars

46. The Baptism of Christ (detail)

47. The Flight into Egypt (detail)

51. The Paradise

54. St. Mary of Egypt (detail)

55. The Samaritan

56. The Entombment
57. The Entombment (detail)
58. The Entombment (detail)

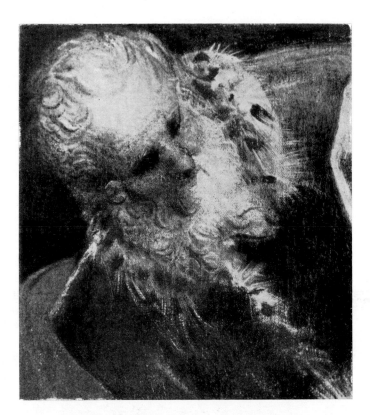

59. The Adoration of the Magi (detail)

60. The Adoration of the Magi (detail)

61. The Last Supper (detail)
62. The Last Supper (detail)

64. Self-portrait

MERIDIANE PUBLISHING HOUSE
BUCHAREST

PRINTED IN ROMANIA